A Special Gift

PRESENTED TO

_____

FROM

_____

The Glory of Christmas

INSPIRATIONAL WRITINGS FROM

Max Lucado

Charles Swindoll

Anne Graham Lotz

Henry & Richard Blackaby

Contents

GOD'S GREATEST GIFT

The Birth of Jesus Christ 8

The Gift of Salvation 17

Forgiveness of Sins 22

Freedom from Guilt 25

Righteousness: Right Living 28

Victory in Life 33

FRIENDSHIP WITH GOD

Adopted Children of the King............... 40

Our Comfort and Power,

    the Holy Spirit 43

The Assurance of God's Love.................. 49

God Is Our Refuge.................................... 54

An Unfailing Friend 58

God's Compassion and Care.................... 62

LIVING BEYOND BELIEF

Transformed into Godliness 68

A Life of Fulfillment 74

Happiness in Christ.................................. 78

The True Meaning of Peace..................... 82

Hope for Today and Tomorrow 85

Joy in Living 89

ALIVE AND GROWING!

Persevering Through

    Good Times and Bad 98

God's Power: Our Potential 102

Growing Up in Christ 106

VICTORIOUS, TODAY & TOMORROW

Power Through Prayer............................ 116

The Word of God to Guide Us............. 123

Friends and Family: The Body of Christ 129

Heaven, Sweet Home 132

Our Hearts Are at Rest 137

the gift

is not from man to God.

IT IS FROM GOD TO MAN...

MAX LUCADO

God's Greatest Gift

The Birth of Jesus Christ

Christmas comes each year to draw people in from the cold.

Like tiny frightened sparrows, shivering in the winter cold, many live their lives on the barren branches of heartbreak, disappointment, and loneliness, lost in thoughts of shame, self-pity, guilt or failure. One blustery day follows another, and the only company they keep is with fellow-strugglers who land on the same branches, confused and unprotected.

We try so hard to attract them into the warmth. Week after week church bells ring. Choirs sing. Preachers preach. Lighted churches send out their beacon. But nothing seems to bring in those who need warmth the most.

Then, as the year draws to a close, Christmas offers its wonderful message. Emmanuel. God with us. He who resided in heaven, co-equal and co-eternal with the Father and the Spirit, willingly descended into our world. He breathed our air, felt our pain, knew our sorrows, and died for our sins. He didn't come to frighten us, but to show us the way to warmth and safety.

CHARLES SWINDOLL | THE FINISHING TOUCH

There is one word that describes the night he came—ordinary.

The sky was ordinary. An occasional guest stirred the leaves and chilled the air. The stars were diamonds sparkling on black velvet. Fleets of clouds floated in front of the moon.

It was a beautiful night—a night worth peeking out your bedroom window to admire—but not really an unusual one. No reason to expect a surprise. Nothing to keep a person awake. An ordinary night with an ordinary sky.

The sheep were ordinary. Some fat. Some scrawny. Some with barrel bellies. Some with twig legs. Common animals. No fleece made of gold. No history makers. No blue-ribbon winners. They were simply sheep—lumpy, sleeping silhouettes on a hillside.

And the shepherds. Peasants they were. Probably wearing all the clothes they owned. Smelling like sheep and looking just as woolly. They were conscientious, willing to spend the night with their flocks. But you won't find their staffs in a museum nor their writings in a library. No one asked their opinion on social justice or the application of the Torah. They were nameless and simple.

An ordinary night with ordinary sheep and ordinary shepherds. And were it not for a God who loves to hook an "extra" on the front of the ordinary, the night would have gone unnoticed. The sheep would have been forgotten, and the shepherds would have slept the night away.

But God dances amidst the common. And that night he did a waltz.

The black sky exploded with brightness. Trees that had been shadows jumped into clarity. Sheep that had been silent became a chorus of curiosity. One minute the shepherd was dead asleep, the next he was rubbing his eyes and staring into the face of an alien.

The night was ordinary no more.

The angel came in the night because that is when lights are best seen and that is when they are most needed. God comes into the common for the same reason.

His most powerful tools are the simplest.

MAX LUCADO

THE APPLAUSE OF HEAVEN

She was probably thirteen or fourteen… The angel's visit had been more than a bit of a surprise—and his announcement more than a little unbelievable… No one could blame Mary for having a question or two. How could I have a child, she wonders, when I have known no man?

Her question, though, reflected her confidence that God would perform the miracle. Mary didn't ask for a sign. She was enquiring how—not if—God was going to perform this miraculous work.

The angel explained that the "Holy Spirit will come upon you" (Luke 1:35) and also told Mary that her relative Elizabeth would be giving birth to a son despite her old age (v. 36). "For with God nothing will be impossible," said the angel in closing.

Mary humbly replied, "Behold the maidservant of the Lord! Let it be to me according to your word" (v. 38).

God's purposes for us far exceed our human abilities to accomplish them. Our efforts can't succeed apart from Him, and that's exactly how God intends it to be.

When He reveals His plans, He is also promising to fulfill them. Trust Him—and remember, with God, nothing is impossible!

HENRY & RICHARD BLACKABY | DISCOVERING GOD'S DAILY AGENDA

FOR WITH GOD *nothing is* impossible.

LUKE 1:37

The Son is the radiance of God's glory and the exact representation of his being, sustaining all things by his powerful word.

HEBREWS 1:3

WHO IS JESUS?

What is there about Him that makes Him so compelling that
    …some of the greatest architectural achievements in
        Europe were built for worship of Him?
    …some of the world's most beautiful art was created
        to honor Him?
    …some of the world's most glorious music was written
        to praise Him?

Jesus claimed to be the Son of God. He claimed to be God walking the earth in a man's body. Do you believe Him?

Who do you say He is?

ANNE GRAHAM LOTZ

MY JESUS IS…EVERYTHING

UNTETHERED BY TIME, [God] sees us all. From the backwoods of Virginia to the business district of London; from the Vikings to the astronauts, from the cave-dwellers to the kings, from the hut-builders to the finger-pointers to the rock-stackers, he sees us. Vagabonds and ragamuffins all, he saw us before we were born.

And he loves what he sees. Flooded by emotion. Overcome by pride, the Starmaker turns to us, one by one, and says, "You are my child. I love you dearly. I'm aware that someday you'll turn from me and walk away. But I want you to know, I've already provided a way back."

And to prove it, he did something extraordinary.

Stepping from the throne, he removed his robe of light and wrapped himself in skin: pigmented, human skin. The light of the universe entered a dark, wet womb. He whom angels worship nestled himself in the placenta of a peasant, was birthed into the cold night, and then slept on cow's hay.

Mary didn't know whether to give him milk or give him praise, but she gave him both since he was, as near as she could figure, hungry and holy.

Joseph didn't know whether to call him Junior or Father. But in the end called him Jesus, since that's what the angel had said and since he didn't have the faintest idea what to name a God he could cradle in his arms.

Don't you think . . . their heads tilted and their minds wondered, "What in the world are you doing, God?" Or, better phrased, "God, what are you doing in the world?"

"Can anything make me stop loving you?" God asks. "Watch me speak your language, sleep on your earth, and feel your hurts. Behold the maker of sight and sound as he sneezes, coughs, and blows his nose. You wonder if I understand how you feel? Look into the dancing eyes of the kid in Nazareth; that's God walking to school. Ponder the toddler at Mary's table; that's God spilling his milk.

"You wonder how long my love will last? Find your answer on a splintered cross, on a craggy hill. That's me you see up there, your maker, your God, nail-stabbed and bleeding. Covered in spit and sin-soaked.

"That's your sin I'm feeling. That's your death I'm dying. That's your resurrection I'm living. That's how much I love you."

MAX LUCADO | IN THE GRIP OF GRACE

The Gift of Salvation

WHAT A GOD!

*It was fitting for Him for
whom are all things and
by whom are all things,
in bringing many sons to
glory, to make the author
of their salvation perfect
through sufferings.*

HEBREWS 2:10

Ponder the achievement of God.
He doesn't condone our sin, nor does he
    compromise his standard.
He doesn't ignore our rebellion,
    nor does he relax his demands.
Rather than dismiss our sin,
    he assumes our sin and, incredibly,
    sentences himself.
God's holiness is honored. Our sin is punished . . .
    and we are redeemed.
God does what we cannot do
    so we can be what we dare not dream:
    perfect before God.

MAX LUCADO | IN THE GRIP OF GRACE

God's plan of salvation has existed since time began. Only He—in His wisdom, love, power, and perfection—could have devised such a deeply compelling yet incredibly costly plan. Only a God as infinitely loving as our God would be willing to let His sinless Son serve as the perfect and acceptable sacrifice for the sin of the human race.

Jesus, our Servant King, submitted Himself to this eternal plan. He allowed Himself to be nailed to the cross and mocked by His creatures because of our sin. By doing this, Christ established a path to God for sinners; He blazed the trail of salvation that countless others could follow. Interestingly, the Greek translated as author in Hebrews 2:10 can also mean captain, pioneer, or pathfinder.

God gave authority over all creation, over every power and authority, to the Servant Messiah who, completely humbling Himself, died on the cross for the sins of mankind. Two thousand years ago with His own Son and today with His children, God exalts the lowly, strengthens the weak, and honors the humble.

HENRY & RICHARD BLACKABY
DISCOVERING GOD'S DAILY AGENDA

He guards the young.

He seeks the stray.

He finds the lost.

He guides the faithful.

He rights the wronged.

He avenges the abused.

He defends the weak.

He comforts the oppressed.

He welcomes the prodigal.

He heals the sick.

He cleanses the dirty.

He beautifies the barren.

He restores the failure.

He mends the broken.

He blesses the poor.

He fills the empty.

He clothes the naked.

He satisfies the hungry.

He elevates the humble.

He forgives the sinner.

He raises the dead!

My Jesus is…everything!

Anne Graham Lotz | My Jesus Is…Everything

IMAGINE COMING to a friend's house who has invited you over to enjoy a meal. You finish the delicious meal and then listen to some fine music and visit for a while. Finally, you stand up and get your coat as you prepare to leave. But before you leave you reach into your pocket and say, "Now, how much do I owe you?" What an insult! You don't do that with someone who has graciously given you a meal. Isn't it strange, though, how this world is running over with people who think there's something they must do to pay God back? Somehow they are hoping God will smile on them if they work real hard and earn his acceptance; but that's an acceptance on the basis of works. That's not the way it is with grace.

And now that Christ has come and died and thereby satisfied the Father's demands on sin, all we need to do is claim his grace by accepting the free gift of eternal life. Period.

He smiles on us because of his Son's death and resurrection.

It's grace, my friend, amazing grace.

CHARLES SWINDOLL
THE GRACE AWAKENING

Forgiveness *of* Sins

Confession does for the soul what preparing the land does for the field. Before the farmer sows the seed he works the acreage, removing the rocks and pulling the stumps. He knows that seed grows better if the land is prepared. Confession is the act of inviting God to walk the acreage of our hearts. "There is a rock of greed over here Father, I can't budge it. And that tree of guilt near the fence? Its roots are long and deep. And may I show you some dry soil, too crusty for seed?" God's seed grows better if the soil of the heart is cleared.

And so the Father and the Son walk the field together; digging and pulling, preparing the heart for fruit. Confession invites the Father to work the soil of the soul.

Confession seeks pardon from God, not amnesty.

Max Lucado | In the Grip of Grace

*Whatever is born of God
overcomes the world.
And this is the victory that
has overcome the world—
our faith.*

1 JOHN 5:4

If you are in Christ . . . you are guaranteed that your sins will be filtered through, hidden in, and screened out by the sacrifice of Jesus. When God looks at you, he doesn't see you; he sees the One who surrounds you. That means that failure is not a concern for you. Your victory is secure. How could you not be courageous?

Picture it this way. Imagine that you are an ice skater in competition. You are in first place with one more round to go. If you perform well, the trophy is yours. You are nervous, anxious, and frightened.

Then, only minutes before your performance, your trainer rushes to you with the thrilling news: "You've already won! The judges tabulated the scores, and the person in second place can't catch you. You are too far ahead. "

Upon hearing that news, how will you feel? Exhilarated!

And how will you skate? Timidly? Cautiously? Of course not. How about courageously and confidently? You bet you will. You will do your best because the prize is yours. You will skate like a champion because that is what you are!

MAX LUCADO | THE APPLAUSE OF HEAVEN

Freedom from Guilt

We have such a High Priest, who is seated at the right hand of the throne of the Majesty in the heavens.

HEBREWS 8:1

To believe we are totally and eternally debt free is seldom easy. Even if we've stood before the throne and heard it from the king himself, we still doubt. As a result, many are forgiven only a little, not because the grace of the king is limited, but because the faith of the sinner is small. God is willing to forgive all. He's willing to wipe the slate completely clean. He guides us to a pool of mercy and invites us to bathe. Some plunge in, but others just touch the surface. They leave feeling unforgiven. . . .

Where the grace of God is missed, bitterness is born. But where the grace of God is embraced, forgiveness flourishes. . . .

The longer we walk in the garden, the more likely we are to smell like flowers. The more we immerse ourselves in grace, the more likely we are to give grace.

MAX LUCADO

IN THE GRIP OF GRACE

THE JEWISH PRIESTS daily entered the sanctuary to burn incense and trim the lamps. Once a week they replaced the showbread. Once a year, on the Day of Atonement, the high priest entered God's presence. Clearly, the old covenant did not provide for full fellowship between God and His people.

The blood of Christ changed that, though. His death on the cross was the perfect and complete sacrifice for humanity's sins. In fact, no sin or offense is so great that Jesus' atonement cannot make you clean and holy.

In addition to offering this forgiveness and cleansing from sin, Jesus is also our Advocate. Seated at the right hand of God—a sign that His sacrificial work is finished—Jesus has constant access to His Father, and He receives everything He asks for on our behalf.

We will face temptations and difficult circumstances. At times our strength may fail and our faith may waiver, but we have this hope: Christ our High Priest forever intercedes for us with the Father. He is victorious over death and sin, and He will bring us victory as well.

HENRY & RICHARD BLACKABY | DISCOVERING GOD'S DAILY AGENDA

Righteousness: Right Living

STOP AND THINK: Upon believing in Jesus Christ's substitutionary death and bodily resurrection, the once-lost sinner is instantly, unconditionally, and permanently "declared 100% righteous." Anything less and we are not righteous . . . we're almost righteous.

If we were declared 99.9% righteous, some verses would have to be rewritten. Like Isaiah 1:18, which might then read: "'Come now, and let us reason together,' says the Lord, 'Though your sins are as scarlet, they will be light pink.'"

Nonsense! The promise of sins forgiven is all or nothing. Eighty percent won't cut it . . . or 90% . . . or 99 and 44/100% . . . or 99.9%. Let's face it, 0.1% is still sinful. I mean, would you drink a gallon of water with only one tiny drop of strychnine in it? Would you feel comfortable having a surgeon cut on you who was wearing almost-sterile gloves?

When our Lord said "It is finished," he meant "finished." The colossal ransom for sin was fully paid. He satisfied the Father's demand.

IT'S QUIET. It's early. My coffee is hot. The sky is still black. The world is still asleep. The day is coming.

In a few moments the day will arrive. It will roar down the track with the rising of the sun. The stillness of the dawn will be exchanged for the noise of the day. The calm of solitude will be replaced by the pounding pace of the human race. The refuge of the early morning will be invaded by decisions to be made and deadlines to be met.

For the next twelve hours I will be exposed to the day's demands. It is now that I must make a choice. Because of Calvary, I'm free to choose. And so I choose.

I CHOOSE LOVE . . .

No occasion justifies hatred; no injustice warrants bitterness. I choose love. Today I will love God and what God loves.

I CHOOSE JOY . . .

I will invite my God to be the God of circumstance. I will refuse the temptation to be cynical . . . the tool of the lazy thinker. I will refuse to see people as anything less than human beings, created by God. I will refuse to see any problem as anything less than an opportunity to see God.

I CHOOSE PEACE . . .

I will live forgiven. I will forgive so that I may live.

I CHOOSE PATIENCE . . .

I will overlook the inconveniences of the world. Instead of cursing the one who takes my place, I'll invite him to do so. Rather than complain that the wait is too long, I will thank God for a moment to pray. Instead of clinching my fist at new assignments, I will face them with joy and courage.

I CHOOSE KINDNESS . . .

I will be kind to the poor, for they are alone. Kind to the rich, for they are afraid. And kind to the unkind, for such is how God has treated me.

I CHOOSE GOODNESS . . .

I will go without a dollar before I take a dishonest one. I will be overlooked before I will boast. I will confess before I will accuse.

I CHOOSE FAITHFULNESS . . .

Today I will keep my promises. My debtors will not regret their trust. My associates will not question my word. My wife will not question my love. And my children will never fear that their father will not come home.

I CHOOSE GENTLENESS . . .

Nothing is won by force. I choose to be gentle. If I raise my voice may it be only in praise. If I clench my fist, may it be only in prayer. If I make a demand, may it be only of myself.

I CHOOSE SELF-CONTROL . . .

I am a spiritual being. After this body is dead, my spirit will soar. I refuse to let what will rot, rule the eternal. I choose self-control. I will be drunk only by joy. I will be impassioned only by my faith. I will be influenced only by God. I will be taught only by Christ.

Love, joy, peace, patience, kindness, goodness, faithfulness, gentleness, and self-control. To these I commit my day. If I succeed, I will give thanks. If I fail, I will seek his grace. And then, when this day is done, I will place my head on my pillow and rest.

MAX LUCADO | WHEN GOD WHISPERS YOUR NAME

For thus says the High and Lofty
One Who inhabits eternity,
whose name is Holy:
"I dwell in the high and holy place,
With him who has a contrite
and humble spirit,
To revive the spirit of the humble,
And to revive the heart
of the contrite ones."

ISAIAH 57:15

IT'S THE MIRACLE of the Incarnation! Our Holy God took on human flesh in the form of Jesus to pay the price for our sin. So perhaps it's no surprise to read here in Isaiah that God reaches down from His throne to people who are humble in heart.

The Almighty God reigns supreme in the universe. He judges humanity with fairness and mercy. He is exalted and righteous above all powers—natural as well as supernatural. He alone is worthy of worship. No wonder He dwells in "the high and holy place."

But that holy place—that place set apart for a special purpose—is not in a heavenly, celestial palace. That holy place where Almighty God chooses to dwell is in the contrite and humble heart of a believer.

We are never more exalted than when we are humble before our Creator and Sovereign King.

HENRY & RICHARD BLACKABY

DISCOVERING GOD'S DAILY AGENDA

Victory
in Life

It is God's gladness. It is sacred delight. And it is this sacred delight that Jesus promises in the Sermon on the Mount. . . .

But this joy is not cheap. What Jesus promises is not a gimmick to give you goose bumps nor a mental attitude that has to be pumped up at pep rallies. No, Matthew 5 describes God's radical reconstruction of the heart.

Observe the sequence. First, we recognize we are in need (we're poor in spirit). Next, we repent of our self-sufficiency (we mourn). We quit calling the shots and surrender control to God (we're meek). So grateful are we for his presence that we yearn for more of him (we hunger and thirst). As we grow closer to him, we become more like him. We forgive others (we're merciful). We change our outlook (we're pure in heart). We love others (we're peace-makers). We endure injustice (we're persecuted).

It's no casual shift of attitude. It is a demolition of the old structure and a creation of the new. The more radical the change, the greater the joy. And it's worth every effort, for this is the joy of God.

MAX LUCADO

THE APPLAUSE OF HEAVEN

HE IS MORE

The Word who was in the beginning
with God is a living Person.

But He is more.

He is the living expression
of what is on God's mind.

But He is more.

He is the living expression
of what is on God's heart.

But He is even more.

He is the very heart of the Almighty God
of the universe laid bare for all to see!

ANNE GRAHAM LOTZ | MY JESUS IS...EVERYTHING

We all like to succeed, don't we? And there is no greater triumph than what Jesus accomplished on the cross: His victory over the power of sin and death enables us to be in relationship with God Almighty, our heavenly Father.

The victorious Christian life is lived out day by day, hour by hour, as we—by the power of God's Spirit—break sinful patterns in our life and seek to obey God. The victorious Christian life is the Spirit's response to our faith.

God gave us the gift of His Holy Spirit, and when we seek to obey God's will, the Spirit's power is released in us. According to Ephesians 1:19–20, that power is the same "mighty power that [God] worked in Christ when He raised Him from the dead and seated Him at His right hand in the heavenly places."

The strength to overcome is a gift of God—and we have a great deal more power than we know. What will you do today to access that power and experience fresh victories in your life?

HENRY & RICHARD BLACKABY
DISCOVERING GOD'S DAILY AGENDA

WHATEVER IS BORN OF GOD

*overcomes the world.
And this is the victory
that has overcome the world—our faith.*

1 JOHN 5:4

Friendship
with
God

Adopted Children
of the King

*Blessed be the God and Father
of our Lord Jesus Christ,
who has blessed us with every
spiritual blessing in the heavenly
places in Christ, just as He chose
us in Him before the foundation
of the world, that we should be
holy and without blame before
Him in love, having predestined
us to adoption as sons by Jesus
Christ to Himself, according to
the good pleasure of His will,
to the praise of the glory of His
grace, by which He made us
accepted in the Beloved.*

EPHESIANS 1:3–6

AS YOUNGSTERS, we neighborhood kids would play street football. The minute we got home from school, we'd drop the books and hit the pavement. The kid across the street had a dad with a great arm and a strong addiction to football. As soon as he'd pull in the driveway from work we'd start yelling for him to come and play ball. He couldn't resist. Out of fairness he'd always ask, "Which team is losing?" Then he would join that team, which often seemed to be mine.

His appearance in the huddle changed the whole ball game. He was confident, strong, and most of all, he had a plan. We'd circle around him, and he'd look at us and say, "OK boys, here is what we are going to do." The other side was groaning before we left the huddle. You see, we not only had a new plan, we had a new leader.

He brought new life to our team. God does precisely the same. We didn't need a new play; we needed a new plan. We didn't need to trade positions; we needed a new player. That player is Jesus Christ, God's firstborn son.

MAX LUCADO

IN THE GRIP OF GRACE

GOD'S GREAT SALVATION is not a one-time, once-and-for-all event for a believer. Experiencing God's salvation is actually a dynamic, lifelong process of implementing all the power, embracing all the love, and fulfilling all the plans He has for you.

"Work out your salvation" means to access all God has made available to you. It is not a command to work for your salvation. It is a call to enter into your relationship with Jesus with all that you are.

We who are privileged to be called the children of God have a choice. We can enjoy our status as adopted and beloved children of the King and know abundant life in Christ, or we can live as spiritual paupers and neglect all that is rightfully ours. It is not enough to know in our minds that we are God's children. That truth must move into our hearts and impact our lifestyles. Don't be like too many of the King's children who choose to live spiritually impoverished lives.

The process of salvation calls for us to apply energy and effort, focus and faith. The Holy Spirit empowers, Jesus embraces us, and God rewards us now and for eternity.

But as many as received Him, to them He gave the right to become children of God, to those who believe in His name....

1 JOHN 1:12

HENRY & RICHARD BLACKABY

DISCOVERING GOD'S DAILY AGENDA

Our Comfort *and* Power, *the* Holy Spirit

The Amplified Bible gives six names that could be equally
translated from the word for "Counselor." Each name,
as defined by Webster's dictionary, describes a different aspect
of the Person of the Holy Spirit. He is our:

COUNSELOR:
One whose profession is to give advice and manage causes.

COMFORTER:
One who relieves another of mental distress.

HELPER:
One who furnishes with relief or support.
One Who is of use and Who waits upon another.

INTERCESSOR:
One who acts between parties to reconcile differences.

ADVOCATE:
One who pleads the cause of another.

STRENGTHENER:
*One who causes another to grow, become stronger,
endure, and resist attacks.*

STANDBY:
One who can be relied upon either for regular use or in emergencies.

CAN YOU IMAGINE how wonderful it would be to have someone with these attributes in your life?

Are you facing a major decision? *Then you need the Counselor.*

Are you distressed today? *Then you need the Comforter.*

Do you need relief from, or support in, your responsibilities?
Then you need the Helper.

Do you have a broken relationship? *Then you need the Intercessor.*

Are you being criticized, falsely accused, misunderstood?
Then you need the Advocate.

Are you constantly defeated by habits of sin?
Then you need the Strengthener.

Are you unprepared for an emergency? *Then you need the Standby.*

The Holy Spirit is everything that Jesus is!

We become Christians because we "received Christ Jesus the Lord." We become empowered and filled with the Spirit as we "walk in him." What fuel is to a car, the Holy Spirit is to the believer. He energizes us to stay the course. He motivates us in spite of the obstacles. He keeps us going when the road gets rough. It is the Spirit who comforts us in our distress, who calms us in times of calamity, who becomes our companion in loneliness and grief, who spurs our "intuition" into action, who fills our minds with discernment when we are uneasy about a certain decision. In short, he is our spiritual fuel. When we attempt to operate without him or to use some substitute fuel, all systems grind to a halt.

CHARLES SWINDOLL | FLYING CLOSER TO THE FLAME

AT SOME POINT we need more than good advice; we need help. Somewhere on this journey home we realize that a fifty-fifty proposition is too little. We need more . . .

We need help. Help from the inside out. The kind of help Jesus promised. "I will ask the Father, and he will give you another Helper to be with you forever—the Spirit of truth. The world cannot accept him, because it does not see him or know him. But you know him because he lives with you and will be in you" (John 14:16–17, emphasis mine).

Note the final words of the verse. And in doing so, note the dwelling place of God—"in you." Not near us. Not above us. Not around us. But in us. In the part of us we don't even know. In the heart no one else has seen. In the hidden recesses of our being dwells, not an angel, not a philosophy, not a genie, but God. Imagine that.

MAX LUCADO

WHEN GOD WHISPERS YOUR NAME

Thoughts are the thermostat that regulates what we accomplish in life. My body responds and reacts to the input from my mind. If I feed my mind upon doubt, disbelief, and discouragement, that is precisely the kind of day my body will experience. If I adjust my thermostat forward to thoughts filled with vision, vitality, and victory, I can count on that kind of day. Thus, you and I become what we think about. . . .

Thoughts, positive or negative, grow stronger when fertilized with constant repetition. That may explain why so many who are gloomy and gray stay in that mood . . . and why those who are cheery and enthusiastic continue to be so. . . .

You need only one foreman in your mental factory: Mr. Triumph is his name. He is anxious to assist you and available to all the members of God's family.

His real name is the Holy Spirit, the Helper.

CHARLES SWINDOLL | THE FINISHING TOUCH

For all who are led by the Spirit of God
are children of God.

ROMANS 8:14 NLT

TO HEAR MANY of us talk, you'd think we didn't believe this verse. You'd think we didn't believe in the Trinity. We talk about the Father and study the Son—but when it comes to the Holy Spirit, we are confused at best and frightened at worst. Confused because we've never been taught. Frightened because we've been taught to be afraid.

May I simplify things a bit? The Holy Spirit is the presence of God in our lives, carrying on the work of Jesus. The Holy Spirit helps us in three directions—inwardly (by granting us the fruits of the Spirit, Galatians 5:22–24), upwardly (by praying for us, Romans 8:26) and outwardly (by pouring God's love into our hearts, Romans 5:5).

MAX LUCADO

WHEN GOD WHISPERS YOUR NAME

The Assurance of God's Love

HE IS THE CREATOR of the universe and the Designer of the human body. He is the Author of salvation history and the Sovereign over world history. He sits enthroned as the ultimate Victor over sin, death, and pain. He keeps planets in their orbits…and your heart beating.

Yet the psalmist portrayed this Almighty God, enthroned in the heavens, as bending down to listen to the entreaty of one of His children. It's amazing that our Almighty God has any thoughts at all toward His creatures. But hear what the psalmist said: "Your thoughts which are toward us cannot be recounted to You in order; if I would declare and speak of them, they are more than can be numbered" (v.17). The fact that God's thoughts toward us are innumerable is more than we can fathom.

God sits exalted above the universe. We are weak and needy creatures. Yet the Lord thinks of us, hears our cries, brings us up out of horrible places, sets our feet on rock, and puts a song of praise in our mouths (vv. 1–3). He is our Help and our Deliverer. Go to Him now with praise…as well as with requests for deliverance and His holy help.

HENRY & RICHARD BLACKABY

DISCOVERING GOD'S DAILY AGENDA

I am poor and needy;
Yet the Lord thinks upon me.

PSALM 40:17

THERE IS NO WAY our little minds can comprehend the love of God. But that didn't keep him from coming. . . .

From the cradle in Bethlehem to the cross in Jerusalem we've pondered the love of our Father. What can you say to that kind of emotion? Upon learning that God would rather die than live without you, how do you react? How can you begin to explain such passion?

MAX LUCADO
IN THE GRIP OF GRACE

FROM A DISTANCE, we dazzle; up close, we're tarnished. Put enough of us together and we may resemble an impressive mountain range. But when you get down into the shadowy crevices . . . the Alps we ain't.

That's why our Lord means so much to us. He is intimately acquainted with all our ways. Darkness and light are alike to him. Not one of us is hidden from his sight. All things are open and laid bare before him: our darkest secret, our deepest shame, our stormy past, our worst thought, our hidden motive, our vilest imagination . . . even our vain attempts to cover the ugly with snow-white beauty.

He comes up so close. He sees it all. He knows our frame. He remembers we are dust.

Best of all, He loves us still.

CHARLES SWINDOLL | THE FINISHING TOUCH

There are many reasons God saves you: to bring glory to himself, to appease his justice, to demonstrate his sovereignty. But one of the sweetest reasons God saved you is because he is fond of you. He likes having you around. He thinks you are the best thing to come down the pike in quite awhile. . .

If God had a refrigerator, your picture would be on it. If he had a wallet, your photo would be in it. He sends you flowers every spring and a sunrise every morning. Whenever you want to talk, he'll listen. He can live anywhere in the universe, and he chose your heart. And the Christmas gift he sent you in Bethlehem?

Face it, friend.

He's crazy about you.

MAX LUCADO
A GENTLE THUNDER

For I know the thoughts that I think toward you, says the LORD, thoughts of peace and not evil, to give you a future and a hope.

JEREMIAH 29:11

53

God Is Our Refuge

He supplies strength to the weary.
He increases power to the faint.
He offers escape to the tempted.

He sympathizes with the hurting.
He saves the hopeless.
He shields the helpless.
He sustains the homeless.

He gives purpose to the aimless.
He gives reason to the meaningless.
He gives fulfillment to our emptiness.
He gives light in the darkness.
He gives comfort in our loneliness.
He gives fruit in our barrenness.
He gives heaven to the hopeless.
He gives life to the lifeless!

My Jesus is…everything!

ANNE GRAHAM LOTZ

MY JESUS IS…EVERYTHING

BEHOLD, A VIRGIN SHALL BE WITH CHILD,
AND BEAR A SON, AND THEY SHALL CALL
HIS NAME IMMANUEL—
WHICH IS TRANSLATED "GOD WITH US."

MATTHEW 1:23

As long as Jesus is one of many options, he is no option.

As long as you can carry your burdens alone, you don't need a burden bearer. As long as your situation brings you no grief, you will receive no comfort. And as long as you can take him or leave him, you might as well leave him, because he won't be taken half-heartedly.

But when you mourn, when you get to the point of sorrow for your sins, when you admit that you have no other option but to cast all your cares on him, and when there is truly no other name that you can call, then cast all your cares on him, for he is waiting in the midst of the storm.

MAX LUCADO | THE APPLAUSE OF HEAVEN

YOU KNOW THE DARK TIMES—those moments when nothing anyone can say or do will change your circumstances or make everything better. Perhaps you've been blessed in troubled times to have someone come sit with you, just be with you. That person's presence was a source of solace, hope, and strength. Similarly, the risen Christ offers His comforting presence to you today.

The word Immanuel appears only once in the New Testament. No one on record ever called Jesus by this name, yet it is one of the most familiar and encouraging designations of our Lord. Quoting Isaiah 7:14, Matthew applied this title to Jesus as God in the flesh. This name affirms the deity of Jesus, and—as it does so—it clearly implies that God is not only present but also personal and approachable.

It has been said that God the Father is for us, God the Son is with us, and God the Spirit is in us. That being true, we can know the hopeful reassurance of God's strength however dark our days may be.

HENRY & RICHARD BLACKABY | DISCOVERING GOD'S DAILY AGENDA

An Unfailing Friend

GOD'S BOOK is a veritable storehouse of promises—over seven thousand of them. Not empty hopes and dreams, not just nice-sounding, eloquently worded thoughts that make you feel warm all over, but promises. Verbal guarantees in writing, signed by the Creator himself, in which he declares he will do or will refrain from doing specific things.

In a world of liars, cheats, deceivers, and con artists, isn't it a relief to know there is Someone you can trust? If he said it, you can count on it.

Unlike the rhetoric of politicians who promise anybody anything they want to hear to get elected, what God says, God does.

CHARLES SWINDOLL
THE FINISHING TOUCH

Therefore the LORD HIMSELF

WILL GIVE YOU A SIGN:

Behold,

the virgin shall conceive and bear a Son,

and shall call His name

IMMANUEL.

ISAIAH 7:14

IT'S NO WONDER, then, that the greatest gift God gives is His presence. His name is Immanuel—God with us.

For God to be with us indicates that He has dealt with our sin. Experiencing His divine presence also means that, no matter who is against us, every resource of heaven is at our disposal. Knowing that He is with us is testimony to His tender love—and nothing can ever separate us from that love.

HENRY & RICHARD BLACKABY | DISCOVERING GOD'S DAILY AGENDA

God's Compassion and Care

Storm clouds gather. Problem is, they're the wrong kind. We need rain desperately, but these clouds hold no rain. We need refreshment and renewal, a kind of inner relief. Like you feel when a sudden cloud cover blocks the burning rays of the sun and blows a cool breeze across the back of your neck. But the storm clouds I refer to bring no such relief…

Storm clouds without rain. War clouds without relief… such clouds not only cast ominous shadows of uneasiness, they breed pessimism….

Lest you forget, [God] is still in charge. As the prophet Nahum stated so confidently: "The Lord is slow to anger and great in power; the Lord will not leave the guilty unpunished. His way is in the whirlwind and the storm, and clouds are the dust of his feet" (Nahum 1:3 NIV)….

When God is in clear focus, His powerful presence eclipses our fears. The clouds become nothing more than "the dust of his feet."

CHARLES SWINDOLL
THE FINISHING TOUCH

WE WORRY. We worry about the IRS and the SAT and the FBI. We worry about education, recreation, and constipation. We worry that we won't have enough money, and when we have money we worry that we won't manage it well. We worry that the world will end before the parking meter expires. We worry what the dog thinks if he sees us step out of the shower. We worry that someday we'll learn that fat-free yogurt was fattening.

Honestly, now. Did God save you so you would fret? Would he teach you to walk just to watch you fall? Would he be nailed to the cross for your sins and then disregard your prayers? Come on. Is Scripture teasing us when it reads, "He has put his angels in charge of you to watch over you wherever you go"? (Psalm 91:11).

I don't think so either.

MAX LUCADO | IN THE GRIP OF GRACE

When his joy invades our lives,

it spills over

into everything we do

and onto everyone we touch.

CHARLES SWINDOLL

Living Beyond Belief

Transformed *into* Godliness

We all, with unveiled face, beholding as in a mirror the glory of the Lord, are being transformed into the same image from glory to glory.

2 CORINTHIANS 3:18

Godliness is something below the surface of a life, deep down in the realm of attitude…an attitude toward God himself.

The longer I think about this, the more I believe that a person who is godly is one whose heart is sensitive toward God, one who takes God seriously. This evidences itself in one very obvious mannerism: the godly individual hungers and thirsts after God. In the words of the psalmist, the godly person has a soul that "pants" for the living god (Psalm 42:1–2).

Godly people possess an attitude of willing submission to God's will and ways. Whatever he says goes. And whatever it takes to carry it out is the very thing the godly desire to do.

CHARLES SWINDOLL | THE FINISHING TOUCH

IT WAS A DIVINE ENCOUNTER that Peter, James, and John never forgot. Jesus led them to a high mountaintop, and there the Lord was "transfigured before them. His face shone like the sun, and His clothes became as white as the light" (Matthew 17:2).

These three disciples were privileged to observe in a dramatic way that Jesus is "the glory of the Lord," the complete personal expression of God. This unfading, eternal glory radiates through believers who are transformed into God's image and who share in His glory.

The Greek word translated "transformed" or "transfigured" means "changed into another form either externally or internally," but this change is not self-generated. Our remodeling into Christlikeness is God's work in us. It begins at salvation, and it happens by the Spirit as we walk with and abide in Christ.

God, by His Spirit, gradually but assuredly conforms you into His image. So learn to live continuously in God's presence. Yield to every change the Spirit seeks to make. Never let a hurried lifestyle disrupt your abiding in Christ.

HENRY & RICHARD BLACKABY
DISCOVERING GOD'S DAILY AGENDA

YOU WANT TO MAKE A DIFFERENCE IN YOUR WORLD?

Live a holy life:

BE FAITHFUL to your spouse.

BE THE ONE at the office who refuses to cheat.

BE THE NEIGHBOR who acts neighborly.

BE THE EMPLOYEE who does the work and doesn't complain.

PAY YOUR BILLS.

DO YOUR PART and enjoy life.

DON'T SPEAK ONE MESSAGE and live another.

*People are watching the way we act
more than they are listening to what we say.*

MAX LUCADO | A GENTLE THUNDER

ANYONE WHO LOVES THE SEA has a romance with it as well as a respect for it. The romance is difficult to describe except by poets—for it defies analysis. The mind moves into another gear as the primeval rhythms of the seashore erode tidy resolutions and hectic deadlines. Time tables, appointments, and schedules are blurred by the salt mist. The thundering waves pull us with a powerful magnetism we cannot resist as we toss our cares and responsibilities to the prevailing winds. . . .

What is hidden in the sea is also hidden in God's wisdom. . . .

Those fathomless truths about him and those profound insights from him produce within us a wisdom that enables us to think with him. Such wisdom comes from his Spirit who, alone, can plumb the depths and reveal his mind.

The hurried, the greedy, the impatient cannot enter into such mysteries. God grants such understanding only to those who wait in silence . . . who respect "the depths of God." It takes time. It calls for solitude.

CHARLES SWINDOLL
THE FINISHING TOUCH

Content. That's the word. A state of heart in which you would be at peace if God gave you nothing more than he already has. Test this question: What if God's only gift to you were his grace to save you. Would you be content? You beg him to save the life of your child. You plead with him to keep your business afloat. You implore him to remove the cancer from your body. What if his answer is, "My grace is enough." Would you be content?

You see, from heaven's perspective, grace is enough. If God did nothing more than save us from hell, could anyone complain? . . . Having been given eternal life, dare we grumble at an aching body? Having been given heavenly riches, dare we bemoan earthly poverty?

Let me be quick to add, God has not left you with "just salvation." If you have eyes to read these words, hands to hold this book, the means to own this volume, he has already given you grace upon grace. The vast majority of us have been saved and then blessed even more!

MAX LUCADO | IN THE GRIP OF GRACE

A Life *of* Fulfillment

God said to Moses,
"I AM WHO I AM....
Say to the Israelites,
'The Lord, the God
of your fathers—
the God of Abraham, the
God of Isaac and
the God of Jacob—
has sent me to you.'"

EXODUS 3:14–15

The Hebrew for Lord, God's name, is YHWH. Translated "I AM" and used about seven thousand times in the Old Testament, this most sublime name of God was whispered by the high priest in the Most Holy Place once a year. Outside of that important occasion, the name was never written or uttered.

YHWH, or Yahweh, speaks of God as "He that always was, always is, and ever is to come." God revealed this name to Moses, and it became the name associated with the covenant between God and His people.

That Old Testament covenant has been fulfilled in the New Testament, enabling you to find forgiveness for your sins and to enjoy an intimate relationship with your heavenly Father. As you live out your faith, you will come to know God as Healer, Protector, Provider, Comforter, and Savior.

Your unique life experiences will reveal God's nature to you in countless personal ways. Ask Him to help you see this very day some of the ways He is revealing His character to you.

HENRY & RICHARD BLACKABY
DISCOVERING GOD'S DAILY AGENDA

WHEN I GAVE IT ALL to Jesus, He accepted it! He has acknowledged that I am not enough in myself to meet anyone else's need. Yet He has blessed what I have given Him, broken and rearranged it to suit Himself until I knew my resources were even more inadequate than I had thought, and He has given me insights into Him and His Word that only He could give.

What is your multitude? Who are the people God wants you to help Him feed? Who are the people you come into contact with who are hungry for the bread of God's Word? And what are your 'loaves and fish'? What very limited and inadequate resources do you have? Wouldn't you like to experience the thrill of participating with Him in the miracle of feeding others with what you have received from Him— and finding that it's enough to satisfy the hunger?

ANNE GRAHAM LOTZ | MY JESUS IS...EVERYTHING

AND MY GOD SHALL SUPPLY ALL YOUR NEED
ACCORDING TO HIS RICHES IN GLORY BY CHRIST JESUS.

PHILIPPIANS 4:19

A piano sits in a room, gathering dust. It is full of the music of the masters, but in order for such strains to flow from it, fingers must strike the keys . . . trained fingers, representing endless hours of disciplined dedication. You do not have to practice. The piano neither requires it nor demands it. If, however, you want to draw beautiful music from the piano, that discipline is required. . . .

You do not have to pay the price to grow and expand intellectually. The mind neither requires it nor demands it. If, however, you want to experience the joy of discovery and the pleasure of plowing new and fertile soil, effort is required.

Light won't automatically shine upon you nor will truth silently seep into your head by means of rocking-chair osmosis.

It's up to you. It's your move.

CHARLES SWINDOLL | THE FINISHING TOUCH

Happiness *in* Christ

BACK WHEN I was in grade school, it was always a special treat when the teacher gave the class permission to do something unusual.

I remember one hot and humid Houston afternoon when she gave everyone permission to go barefoot after lunch. We got to pull off our socks, stick 'em in our sneakers, and wiggle our toes all we wanted to. During the afternoon recess that extra freedom added great speed to our softball game on the playground. . . .

Isn't it strange then, now that you and I are grown and have become Christians, how reluctant we are to give ourselves permission to do . . . to think . . . to say . . . to buy and enjoy . . . or to be different and not worry about who may say what?

Even though our God has graciously granted us permission to be free, to have liberty, to break the chains of rigidity, and to enjoy so much of this life, many in his family seldom give themselves permission.

CHARLES SWINDOLL
THE FINISHING TOUCH

He discharges the debtors.
He delivers the captives.
He defends the feeble.
He blesses the young.
He serves the unfortunate.
He regards the aged.
He rewards the diligent.
He beautifies the meek.

He is the key to knowledge.
He is the wellspring of wisdom.
He is the doorway of deliverance.
He is the pathway to peace.
He is the roadway of righteousness.
He is the gateway to glory.
He is the highway to happiness.

My Jesus is…everything!

ANNE GRAHAM LOTZ | MY JESUS IS…EVERYTHING

*Therefore if the Son
makes you free,
you shall be free indeed.*

JOHN 8:36

IT OCCURRED TO ME last week that there is a practical reason Thanksgiving always precedes Christmas: It sets in motion the ideal mental attitude to carry us through the weeks in between. In other words, a sustained spirit of gratitude makes the weeks before Christmas a celebration rather than a marathon.

Maybe these few thoughts will stimulate you to give God your own thanks in greater abundance.

Thank You Lord…

> *for Your sovereign control over our circumstances,*
> *for Your holy character in spite of our sinfulness,*
> *for Your commitment to us even when we wander astray,*
> *for Your Word that gives us direction,*
> *for Your love that holds us close,*
> *for Your gentle compassion in our sorrows,*
> *for Your consistent faithfulness through our highs and lows,*
> *for Your understanding when we are confused,*
> *for Your Spirit that enlightens our eyes,*
> *for Your grace that removes our guilt.*

CHARLES SWINDOLL

THE FINISHING TOUCH

The True Meaning of Peace

I myself always strive to have a conscience
without offense toward God and men.

ACTS 24:16

ONE WISE SAINT made this observation with a smile: "It would be very humbling to realize how infrequently other people are thinking of you—because they're too busy thinking about what you may be thinking of them!"

You can't control what other people think of you, but you can live at peace whatever their thoughts might be. You can know peace because no matter what happens *to* you, you have control over what happens *in* you.

What happens inside you is determined by the condition of your heart. A heart at peace is a clean heart, a repentant heart that has experienced God's forgiveness and been cleansed (1 John 1:8–9). A contentious spirit comes with not allowing the Holy Spirit to rule in one's life.

So, like Paul, prayerfully and carefully live so as not to offend God or people. Having had your heart cleansed, be willing to humble yourself before God, to ask forgiveness when necessary, and, if doing so will bring reconciliation with others, even to overlook transgressions. Strive to be at peace with everyone and choose not to take offense at others. A clear conscience is priceless.

HENRY & RICHARD BLACKABY
DISCOVERING GOD'S DAILY AGENDA

Somewhere, miles away, crops push their way toward harvest and waves roar and tumble onto shore. Windswept forests sing their timeless songs, and desert animals scurry in the shadows of cactus and rock.

Within a matter of hours night will fall, the dark sky will glitter with moon and stars, and sleep will force itself upon us. Life will continue on uninterrupted. Appreciated or not, the canvas of nature will go on being painted by the fingers of God.

In the midst of the offensive noise of our modern world—the people, the cars, the sounds, the smog, the heat, the pressures—there stand those reminders of His deep peace.

The running wave, the flowing air, the quiet earth, the shining stars, the gentle night, the healing light... and from each, the blessing of the deep peace of Christ to you, to me.

CHARLES SWINDOLL | THE FINISHING TOUCH

Peace I leave with you, My peace I give to you;
not as the world gives do I give to you.
Let not your heart be troubled, neither let it be afraid.

JOHN 14:27

Hope *for* Today and Tomorrow

His office is manifold, and His promise is sure.
His life is matchless, and His goodness is limitless.
His mercy is enough, and His grace is sufficient.
His reign is righteous, His yoke is easy, and His burden is light.
He is indestructible. He is indescribable.
He is incomprehensible. He is inescapable.
He is invincible. He is irresistible. He is irrefutable.

My Jesus is…everything!

ANNE GRAHAM LOTZ
MY JESUS IS…EVERYTHING

When my soul fainted within me,
I remembered the LORD;
And my prayer went up to You, into Your holy temple.

JONAH 2:7

SOMEONE ONCE COUNTED all the promises in the Bible and came up with an amazing figure of almost 7500. Among that large number are some specific promises servants can claim today. Believe me, there are times when the only thing that will keep you going is a promise from God that your work is not in vain.

When we have done what was needed, but were ignored, misunderstood, or forgotten . . . we can be sure it was not in vain.

When we did what was right, with the right motive, but received no credit, no acknowledgment, not even a "thank you" . . . we have God's promise that "we shall reap."

When any servant has served and given and sacrificed and then willingly stepped aside for God to receive the glory, our heavenly Father promises he will receive back.

CHARLES SWINDOLL | THE FINISHING TOUCH

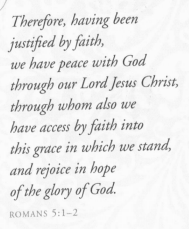

*Therefore, having been
justified by faith,
we have peace with God
through our Lord Jesus Christ,
through whom also we
have access by faith into
this grace in which we stand,
and rejoice in hope
of the glory of God.*

ROMANS 5:1–2

Bittersweet is a word that aptly describes the hard times when we turn to God and find Him to be all that we need.

Think about those times when you've had nowhere else to turn but the Lord—and you weren't even sure He was listening or if He even cared. That was a bitter starting point, but the sweetness came in time. Oh, the circumstances may not have changed—the marriage may not have been rehabilitated, the child may not yet be walking with the Lord again, the chemo may not have done what you'd hoped and prayed for—but everything was different because of the sweet presence of your heavenly Father.

It's all too easy to forget that we need Him, isn't it? It's generally during the crises more than in the peaceful times that we remember our dependence on God and prayerfully turn to Him. When it feels as if our soul faints within us—as Jonah's did—we remember our all-powerful, ever-faithful God and lift our prayers to Him.

Whether your current circumstances are sweet or bitter or somewhere in between, lift up your voice to God today.

HENRY & RICHARD BLACKABY | DISCOVERING GOD'S DAILY AGENDA

Joy *in* Living

THE FIRST STEP to joy is a plea for help, an acknowledgment of moral destitution, an admission of inward paucity. Those who taste God's presence have declared spiritual bankruptcy and are aware of their spiritual crisis. Their cupboards are bare. Their pockets are empty. Their options are gone. They have long since stopped demanding justice; they are pleading for mercy.

They don't brag; they beg.

They ask God to do for them what they can't do without him. They have seen how holy God is and how sinful they are and have agreed with Jesus' statement, "Salvation is impossible."

Oh, the irony of God's delight—born in the parched soil of destitution rather than the fertile ground of achievement.

It's a different path, a path we're not accustomed to taking. We don't often declare our impotence. Admission of failure is not usually admission into joy. Complete confession is not commonly followed by total pardon. But then again, God has never been governed by what is common.

MAX LUCADO | THE APPLAUSE OF HEAVEN

Those who sow in tears
Shall reap in joy.
He who continually
goes forth weeping...
Shall doubtless come
again with rejoicing...

PSALM 126:5–6

AREN'T THESE VERSES ENCOURAGING? From tears to joy, from weeping to rejoicing—that's a radical transformation. The Almighty God, for whom nothing is impossible; the all-loving God, whose plans for you are plans for good; the all-wise God who knows what is best for each one of His children—our God has the power to bring beauty from ashes. He brings hope in the most difficult circumstances.

The promises found in these verses characterize the Lord and the transforming work He can do in your heart and life. God can transform your tears into joy. Whatever reasons for those tears, we who serve the Lord can always have hope in Him. We know that He can completely transform even the worst situation; we know that His presence can turn tears to joy and sorrow into celebration.

The Crucifixion preceded the Resurrection. That was God's power at work. Whatever loss or death, whatever pain or struggle you're dealing with, know that God can bring into your situation new life, genuine joy, and heartfelt rejoicing. That's the God we serve.

HENRY & RICHARD BLACKABY

DISCOVERING GOD'S DAILY AGENDA

Seren-dip-ity—the dip of the serene into the common responsibilities of life. Serendipity occurs when something beautiful breaks into the monotonous and the mundane.

A serendipitous life is marked by "surprisability" and spontaneity. When we lose our capacity for either, we settle into life's ruts. We expect little, and we're seldom disappointed.

Though I have walked with God for several decades, I must confess I still find much about Him incomprehensible and mysterious. But this much I know: He delights in surprising us. He dots our pilgrimage from earth to heaven with amazing serendipities. . . .

Your situation may be as hot and barren as a desert or as forlorn and meaningless as a wasteland. You may be tempted to think, "There's no way!" when someone suggests things could change.

All I ask is that you . . . be on the lookout. God may very well be planning a serendipity in your life.

Charles Swindoll
The Finishing Touch

O Lord, our Lord,

How excellent is Your name in all the earth,

You who set Your glory above the heavens!

PSALM 8:1

WANT TO SEE A MIRACLE? Plant a word of love heartdeep in a person's life. Nurture it with a smile and a prayer, and watch what happens.

An employee gets a compliment. A wife receives a bouquet of flowers. A cake is baked and carried next door. A widow is hugged. A gas-station attendant is honored. A preacher is praised.

Sowing seeds of peace is like sowing beans. You don't know why it works; you just know it does. Seeds are planted, and topsoils of hurt are shoved away.

Don't forget the principle.

Never underestimate the power of a seed.

MAX LUCADO | THE APPLAUSE OF HEAVEN

Key to understanding the psalmist's words of praise is knowing that God's name reflects His character. For instance, the name El Shaddai means "All-sufficient" or "Almighty One." El Elyon means "the Most High God" and refers to God's supremacy and sovereignty. The names of God reveal who He is.

Here the psalmist was truly delighting in who God is and what He is like. Look at the picture of God's amazing creation that the psalmist painted—"When I consider Your heavens, the work of your fingers, the moon and the stars, which You have ordained"—and hear how he was humbled and awed by what he saw: "What is man that You are mindful of him, and the son of man that You visit him?" (vv. 3–4).

Within the majestic expanse of the universe, we are insignificant specks. Yet our infinite God sees us, knows us intimately, and loves us ceaselessly. Such divine consideration is truly beyond our comprehension.

O Lord, our Lord, your love for me is truly amazing! Teach me to delight in You.

HENRY & RICHARD BLACKABY
DISCOVERING GOD'S DAILY AGENDA

SERVANTHOOD IMPLIES DILIGENCE, FAITHFULNESS, LOYALTY, AND HUMILITY.

Servants don't compete . . . or grandstand . . .
or polish their image . . . or grab the limelight.
They know their job, they admit their limitations,
they do what they do quietly and consistently.

Servants cannot control anyone or everything,
and they shouldn't try.

Servants cannot change or "fix" people.

Servants cannot explain many of the great things that happen.

Servants cannot meet most folks' expectations.

Servants cannot concern themselves with who gets the credit. . . .

Let's serve . . . in the name of Jesus.

CHARLES SWINDOLL | THE FINISHING TOUCH

With each new dawn,
life delivers a package
to your front door,
rings your doorbell,
and runs.

CHARLES SWINDOLL

Alive and Growing

Persevering
Through Good Times
and Bad

What kinds of trials have caused you to suffer grief?
Could it be God has given you a platform of suffering from which you
can be a witness of His power and grace to those who are watching?
Because if we always feel good
    and look good
    and lead a good life;
    if our kids always behave
    and our boss is always pleased
    and our home is always orderly
    and our friends are always available
    and our bank account is always sufficient
    and our car always starts
    and our bodies always feel good
and we are patient and kind and thoughtful and happy and loving...
others shrug because under those kinds of circumstances, they're capable
of being that way too.

On the other hand, if we have a splitting headache,
    the kids are screaming,
    the phone is ringing,
    the boss is yelling,
    the super is burning,
yet we are patient, kind, thoughtful, happy, and loving...the world
sits up and takes notice. The world knows that kind of behavior is not
natural. It's supernatural.

ANNE GRAHAM LOTS | MY JESUS IS...EVERYTHING

Take from us our wealth and we are hindered.

Take our health and we are handicapped.

Take our purpose and we are slowed, temporarily confused.

But take away our hope, and we are plunged into deep darkness . . . stopped dead in our tracks, paralyzed. Wondering, "Why?" Asking, "How much longer? Will this darkness ever end? Does he know where I am?"

Then the Father says, "That's far enough," and how sweet it is! Like blossoms in the snow, long-awaited color returns to our life. The stream, once frozen, starts to thaw. Hope revives and washes over us.

Inevitably, spring follows winter. Every year. Yes, including this one. Barren days, like naked limbs, will soon be clothed with fresh life. Do you need that reminder today? Are you ready for some sunshine on your shoulders . . . a few green sprouts poking up through all that white? A light at the end of your tunnel?

Look! There it is in the distance. It may be tiny, but it's there.

CHARLES SWINDOLL

THE FINISHING TOUCH

Yet I will rejoice in the LORD, I will joy in the God of my salvation.

HABAKKUK 3:18

BECAUSE IT IS SHORT, life is packed with challenging possibilities. Because it is uncertain, it's filled with challenging adjustments. I'm convinced that's much of what Jesus meant when he promised us an abundant life. Abundant with challenges, running over with possibilities, filled with opportunities to adapt, shift, alter, and change. Come to think of it, that's the secret of staying young. It is also the path that leads to optimism and motivation.

With each new dawn, life delivers a package to your front door, rings your doorbell, and runs. Each package is cleverly wrapped in paper with big print. One package reads: "Watch out. Better worry about this!" Another: "Danger. This will bring fear!" And another: "Impossible. You'll never handle this one!"

When you hear that ring tomorrow morning, try something new. Have Jesus Christ answer the door for you.

CHARLES SWINDOLL | THE FINISHING TOUCH

God's Power: Our Potential

WHY DOES GOD wait until the money is gone? Why does he wait until the sickness has lingered? Why does he choose to wait until the other side of the grave to answer the prayers for healing?

I don't know. I only know his timing is always right. I can only say he will do what is best. "God will always give what is right to his people who cry to him night and day, and he will not be slow to answer them" (Luke 18:7).

Though you hear nothing, he is speaking. Though you see nothing, he is acting. With God there are no accidents. Every incident is intended to bring us closer to him.

MAX LUCADO
A GENTLE THUNDER

I thank my God upon every remembrance of you…being confident that He who has begun a good work in you will complete it until the day of Christ Jesus.

PHILIPPIANS 1:6

GOD LOVED YOU, chose you, drew you, enlightened you, and saved you—and He is not finished with you yet.

God desires that your foremost pursuit would be your deepening relationship with Jesus Christ. Purpose and passion, peace and contentment would then characterize your life. Consider that the Holy Spirit gave the apostle Paul joy even while he was in prison. The same joy is available to you whatever your present circumstances.

Another one of God's desires for you is to bring you into the center of His activity according to His kingdom purpose for your life. So stand before Him with a heart of ready obedience. After all, God alone knows what you will become as you serve Him according to His plan.

Finally, be encouraged to know that God continues to be at work in you. The challenge you face is to walk with Him and to completely release your self to His will. You can trust your day-to-day life—as well as your eternal future—to Him.

HENRY & RICHARD BLACKABY | DISCOVERING GOD'S DAILY AGENDA

We admire pioneers . . . so long as we can just read about them, not finance their journeys. We applaud explorers. . . but not if it means we have to load up and travel with them. Creative ideas are fine . . . "but don't get carried away," we warn. . . .

When it came time for God to send his Son to earth, he did not send him to the palace of some mighty king. He was conceived in the womb of an unwed mother—a virgin!—who lived in the lowly village of Nazareth.

In choosing those who would represent Christ and establish his church, God picked some of the most unusual individuals imaginable: unschooled fishermen, a tax collector(!), a mystic, a doubter, and a former Pharisee who had persecuted Christians. He continued to pick some very unusual persons down through the ages. In fact, he seems to delight in such surprising choices to this very day.

So, let God be God. Expect the unexpected.

CHARLES SWINDOLL
THE FINISHING TOUCH

Growing Up *in* Christ

HOW DO YOU WANT TO BE remembered? How about for not "grow [ing] weary in doing good"? That would indeed be a life well spent.

Life on earth is short and eternity is long. So serve the Lord with all your heart and make your life count.

- *Love generously.* God designed love to have a powerful impact on human relationships. Whether it is expressed by forgiving, addressing a person's needs, sharing the Good News, or encouraging the weary, love can change a life forever.
- *Share Christian kindness.* Kindness has been defined as "God's love expressed in practical ways." It is intentionally sharing the love He has given us. The condition of our relationship with God is reflected in how compassionate, tender, generous, and forgiving we are.
- *Practice hospitality.* The character of the Christian home can do much to prove the relevance and attractiveness of the Christian message.
- *Serve the church.* God's work in believers' lives is evident when they love the body of Christ.

God has given you life, so—by His grace and in His power—persevere and live it well.

HENRY & RICHARD BLACKABY

DISCOVERING GOD'S DAILY AGENDA

Do not grow weary in doing good.

2 THESSALONIANS 3:13

SPIRITUAL LIFE COMES FROM THE SPIRIT! Your parents may have given you genes, but God gives you grace. Your parents may be responsible for your body, but God has taken charge of your soul. You may get your looks from your mother, but you get eternity from your Father, your heavenly Father. . . .

God has not left you adrift on a sea of heredity. . . . You cannot control the way your forefathers responded to God. But you can control the way you respond to him. The past does not have to be your prison. You have a voice in your destiny. You have a say in your life. You have a choice in the path you take.

Choose well and someday—generations from now—your grandchildren and great-grandchildren will thank God for the seeds you sowed.

MAX LUCADO

WHEN GOD WHISPERS YOUR NAME

When it comes to irritations, I've found that it helps if I remember that I am not in charge of my day . . . God is. And while I'm sure he wants me to use my time wisely, he is more concerned with the development of my character and the cultivation of the qualities that make me Christlike within. One of his preferred methods of training is through adjustments to irritations.

A perfect illustration? The oyster and its pearl.

Pearls are the products of irritation. This irritation occurs when the shell of the oyster is invaded by an alien substance like a grain of sand. When that happens, all the resources within the tiny, sensitive oyster rush to the irritated spot and begin to release healing fluids that otherwise would have remained dormant. By and by the irritant is covered—by a pearl. Had there been no irritating interruption, there could have been no pearl.

No wonder our heavenly home has pearly gates to welcome the wounded and bruised who have responded correctly to the sting of irritations.

CHARLES SWINDOLL | THE FINISHING TOUCH

I thank Christ Jesus our Lord who has enabled me,
because He counted me faithful,
putting me into the ministry.

1 TIMOTHY 1:12

THOSE WHOM God calls to a specific task He always enables.

When the Lord sees we have been faithful in a little, He gives us more—and His "more" will always stretch us. We would find it easier to continue being faithful where we already are than to go to the next level in our walk with God, but then we would stop growing. So God puts us in places of greater service where we will fail unless we develop a greater trust in Him than we have ever had before.

But along with every challenging call comes God's perfect enabling. He is prepared to meet every need we will face as we step out in obedience and faith. He will grant us the strength we need to match every demand. He will bestow the wisdom we need to navigate every decision.

It is an awesome experience to realize that Almighty God is personally equipping you to serve Him. So if God is calling you to a new assignment, be encouraged! You are about to experience God in ways you have never known before.

HENRY & RICHARD BLACKABY | DISCOVERING GOD'S DAILY AGENDA

HERE IS WHAT WE WANT TO KNOW. We want to know how long God's love will endure. . . . Does God really love us forever? Not just on Easter Sunday when our shoes are shined and our hair is fixed. We want to know . . . how does God feel about me when I'm a jerk? Not when I'm peppy and positive and ready to tackle world hunger. Not then. I know how he feels about me then. Even I like me then.

I want to know how he feels about me when I snap at anything that moves, when my thoughts are gutter-level, when my tongue is sharp enough to slice a rock. How does he feel about me then? . . .

Can anything separate us from the love Christ has for us?

God answered our question before we asked it. So we'd see his answer, he lit the sky with a star. So we'd hear it, he filled the night with a choir; and so we'd believe it, he did what no man had ever dreamed. He became flesh and dwelt among us.

He placed his hand on the shoulder of humanity and said, "You're something special."

MAX LUCADO
IN THE GRIP OF GRACE

JESUS KNOWS:

the small secrets of your heart,
the unspoken dreams of your imagination,
the unrevealed thoughts of your mind,
the emotional shards of your feelings,
the paralyzing fears for your future,
the bitter resentments of your past,
the joys and heartaches,
the pleasures and pain,
the successes and failures,
the honors and humiliations,
the deeds and the doubts.

He knows all about you,
inside and out,
past, present, and future.

ANNE GRAHAM LOTZ | MY JESUS IS...EVERYTHING

I will praise you,
FOR I AM FEARFULLY AND
WONDERFULLY MADE.
Marvelous
are Your works,
AND THAT MY SOUL
KNOWS VERY WELL.

PSALM 139:14

Victorious, Today & Tomorrow

Power Through Prayer

Do you want to know how to deepen your prayer life? Pray. Don't prepare to pray. Just pray. Don't read about prayer. Just pray. Don't attend a lecture on prayer or engage in discussion about prayer. Just pray.

Posture, tone, and place are personal matters. Select the form that works for you. But don't think about it too much. Don't be so concerned about wrapping the gift that you never give it. Better to pray awkwardly than not at all.

And if you feel you should only pray when inspired, that's okay. Just see to it that you are inspired every day.

Max Lucado

When God Whispers Your Name

WHAT PRESSURE HAVE YOU recently been under? Do you feel emotionally drained, physically exhausted, and spiritually deplete as well? Jesus sees and understands your needs.

Jesus saw the physical, emotional, and spiritual needs of His friends and knew the solution was a time of quiet rest and reflection. And He knows the solution is the same for you and me today. So He invites, us, as He did His disciples, "Come with Me by yourself to a quiet place and get some rest."

Often when I am under stress and pressure, I feel one of my greatest needs is to get a good night's sleep. But I've found that physical rest alone is not enough to revive my flagging spirit. I need the spiritual revival that comes from spending quiet time alone with Jesus in prayer and in thoughtful meditation on His Word.

ANNE GRAHAM LOTZ
MY JESUS IS…EVERYTHING

The Scriptures are replete with references to the value of waiting for the Lord and spending time with him.

When we do, the debris we have gathered during the hurried, busy hours of our day gets filtered out, not unlike the silt that settles where a river widens. With the debris out of the way, we are able to see things more clearly and feel God's nudgings more sensitively.

David frequently underscored the benefits of solitude.

I am certain he first became acquainted with this discipline as he kept his father's sheep. Later, during those tumultuous years when King Saul was borderline insane and pursuing him out of jealousy, David found his time with God not only a needed refuge but his means of survival. . . .

God still longs to speak to waiting hearts . . . hearts that are quiet before him.

CHARLES SWINDOLL | THE FINISHING TOUCH

Confess your trespasses to one another,
and pray for one another, that you may be healed.
The effective, fervent prayer of a righteous man avails much.

IT'S NOT DIFFICULT TO SEE why these two statements are found side by side in Scripture....

First, we're called to confess our sin. We're to openly acknowledge our trespasses, fully agree with God that we've done wrong, and then accept what is to come as a result of our sins. Confessing in a public fashion—as James calls us to do—provides an opportunity for personal cleansing as well as corporate instruction and accountability.

After hearing this call to confession, we read about the prayers of "a righteous man." When we confess our sin and ask forgiveness, we become holy due to Christ's death on the cross for that sin. Then, having been cleansed of our sin, we can pray effectively as we pray fervently.

You don't have to be a spiritual giant before God answers your prayer. But God does expect you to enter His presence with a keen sense of your need for His involvement in your life. The heartfelt prayers of a desperate sinner gain God's immediate attention.

So pray for forgiveness, pray fervently, and watch God work.

HENRY & RICHARD BLACKABY | DISCOVERING GOD'S DAILY AGENDA

NOW IT IS IMPORTANT to remember that some of the most profound ministries of the Spirit of God are not public or loud or large. Sometimes his most meaningful touch on our lives comes when we are all alone.

I urge you to include in your schedule time to be alone with God. I am fortunate to live within ninety minutes of the mountains . . . and less than forty-five minutes from the beach. Those are great places to commune with God. You do have places where you can get away for a long walk, don't you? I hope it's in a wooded area. The gentle breeze blowing through the forest is therapeutic. Sometimes just being alone out in God's marvelous creation is all that's needed for the scales to be removed from your eyes and for you to silence the harassment and the noise of your day and begin to hear from God.

CHARLES SWINDOLL
FLYING CLOSER TO THE FLAME

A SMALL CATHEDRAL outside Bethlehem marks the supposed birthplace of Jesus. Behind a high altar in the church is a cave, a little cavern lit by silver lamps.

You can enter the main edifice and admire the ancient church. You can also enter the quiet cave where a star embedded in the floor recognizes the birth of the King. There is one stipulation, however. You have to stoop. The door is so low you can't go in standing up.

The same is true of the Christ. You can see the world standing tall, but to witness the Savior, you have to get on your knees.

MAX LUCADO | THE APPLAUSE OF HEAVEN

The Word *of* God *to* Guide Us

All Scripture is given
by inspiration of God,
and is profitable for doctrine,
for reproof, for correction,
for instruction in righteousness…

2 TIMOTHY 3:16

PAINTERS CAN BE INSPIRED by the sunset. Poets can be inspired by the person they love. Young people can be inspired by great athletes. But the inspiration God provided the writers of Scripture is quite different.

The Greek behind inspiration means "God-breathed." God didn't merely spark a good idea, fill a heart to overflowing, or fuel a writer's effort. Instead, God—through His Holy Spirit—influenced men's minds in a way that made them His agents for the infallible communication of God's revelation.

The Scriptures, although penned by the hands of men, are the very Word of God. To fully and accurately understand Scripture's truths, then, we must receive illumination or enlightenment by the Holy Spirit, the divine quickening of the human mind. Only the Holy Spirit can enable us to understand the truth that has been revealed and communicated by the power of God. Before you open the Bible, ask the Spirit to open your mind and heart to recognize and understand God's wisdom.

Also, always open your Bible with trembling for you are about to encounter God's holy, life-changing, inspired Word.

HENRY & RICHARD BLACKABY
DISCOVERING GOD'S DAILY AGENDA

THERE IS SOMETHING grand about old things that are still in good shape. Old furniture, rich with the patina of age and history, is far more intriguing than the uncomfortable, modern stuff. When you sit on it or eat off it or sleep in it, your mind pictures those in previous centuries who did the same in a world of candlelight, oil lamps, buggies, outhouses, and potbelly stoves. Each scrape or dent holds a story you wish you knew. . . .

The Bible is old also—ancient, in fact. Its timeless stories have for centuries shouted, "You can make it! Don't quit . . . don t give up!" Its truths, secure and solid as stone, say, "I'm still here, waiting to be claimed and applied." Whether it's a prophet's warning, a patriarch's prayer, a poet's psalm, or a preacher's challenging reminder. The Book of books lives on, offering us new vistas. . . .

Though ancient, it has never lost its relevance. Though battered, no one has ever improved on its content. Though old, it never fails to offer something pure, something wise, something new.

CHARLES SWINDOLL | THE FINISHING TOUCH

Knowing God is more than just being saved or being born again, just as knowing my husband is more than just saying marriage vows at the wedding altar. Knowing God involves an intimate, personal relationship that is developed over time through prayer and getting answer to prayer, through Bible study and applying its teaching to our lives, through obedience and experiencing the power of God, through moment-by-moment filling of the Holy Spirit.

God gives me peace and joy within as I put myself in His hands, trusting Him to infuse my life with His love.

Anne Graham Lotz
My Jesus Is...Everything

DISCIPLINE IS EASY for me to swallow. Logical to assimilate. Manageable and appropriate.

But God's grace? Anything but. Examples? How much time do you have?

David the psalmist becomes David the voyeur, but by God's grace becomes David the psalmist again.

Peter denied Christ before he preached Christ.

Zacchaeus, the crook. The cleanest part of his life was the money he'd laundered. But Jesus still had time for him. . . .

Story after story. Prayer after prayer. Surprise after surprise.

Seems that God is looking more for ways to get us home than for ways to keep us out. I challenge you to find one soul who came to God seeking grace and did not find it.

MAX LUCADO

WHEN GOD WHISPERS YOUR NAME

Friends and Family:
The Body of Christ

NOBODY IS A WHOLE CHAIN. Each one is a link. But take away one link and the chain is broken.

Nobody is a whole team. Each one is a player. But take away one player and the game is forfeited.

Nobody is a whole orchestra. Each one is a musician. But take away one musician and the symphony is incomplete. . . .

You guessed it. We need each other. You need someone and someone needs you. Isolated islands we're not.

To make this thing called life work, we gotta lean and support. And relate and respond. And give and take. And confess and forgive. And reach out and embrace. And release and rely. . . .

Since none of us is a whole, independent, self-sufficient, superb-capable, all-powerful hotshot, let's quit acting like we are. Life's lonely enough without our playing that silly role.

The game's over. Let's link up.

CHARLES SWINDOLL | THE FINISHING TOUCH

ADAM	knew Him as a beloved Father,
EVE	knew Him as the original Homemaker,
NOAH	knew Him as the Refuge from the storm.
ABRAHAM	knew Him as a Friend.
MOSES	knew Him as the Redeemer.
RAHAB	knew Him as the gracious Savior.
DAVID	knew Him as his Shepherd.
ELIJAH	knew Him as the Almighty.
DANIEL	knew Him as the Lion Tamer.
MARY	Magdalene knew Him as the Bondage Breaker.
MARTHA	knew Him as the Promise Keeper.
LAZARUS	knew Him as the Resurrection and the Life.
BARTIMAEUS	knew Him as the Light of the World.
JOHN	knew Him as the glorious King upon the throne.

Surely you and I can know Him too!

ANNE GRAHAM LOTZ

MY JESUS IS…EVERYTHING

Heaven, Sweet Home

THERE DWELLS INSIDE YOU, deep within, a tiny whippoorwill. Listen.

You will hear him sing.

His aria mourns the dusk. His solo signals the dawn.

It is the song of the whippoorwill.

He will not be silent until the sun is seen.

We forget he is there, so easy is he to ignore. Other animals of the heart are larger, noisier, more demanding, more imposing.

But none is so constant.

Other creatures of the soul are more quickly fed. More simply satisfied. We feed the lion who growls for power. We stroke the tiger who demands affection. We bridle the stallion who bucks control.

But what do we do with the whippoorwill who yearns for eternity?

For that is his song. That is his task. Out of the gray he sings a golden song. Perched in time he chirps a timeless verse. Peering through pain's shroud, he sees a painless place. Of that place he sings.

And though we try to ignore him, we cannot. He is us, and his song is ours. Our heart song won't be silenced until we see the dawn.

"God has planted eternity in the hearts of men" (Ecclesiastes 3:10 TLB), says the wise man. But it doesn't take a wise person to know that people long for more than earth. When we see pain, we yearn. When we see hunger, we question why. Senseless deaths. Endless tears, needless loss. Where do they come from? Where will they lead?

Isn't there more to life than death?

And so sings the whippoorwill.

Unhappiness on earth cultivates a hunger for heaven. By gracing us with a deep dissatisfaction, God holds our attention. The only tragedy, then, is to be satisfied prematurely. To settle for earth. To be content in a strange land. To intermarry with the Babylonians and forget Jerusalem.

We are not happy here because we are not at home here. We are not happy here because we are not supposed to be happy here. We are "like foreigners and strangers in this world" (1 Peter 2:11). . . .

And you will never be completely happy on earth simply because you were not made for earth. Oh, you will have your moments of joy. You will catch glimpses of light. You will know moments or even days of peace. But they simply do not compare with the happiness that lies ahead.

MAX LUCADO
WHEN GOD WHISPERS YOUR NAME

I saw a new heaven and a new earth,
for the first heaven and the first earth had passed away.

REVELATION 21:1

OUR EARTH IS PERISHING.... We who dwell here suffer from illness, natural catastrophes, and evil.... Even the righteous grow weary of living in a place so contrary to their values.... But the day is coming when God will create a new heaven and earth, and His creation won't simply be a newer model. God will not merely reform our present situation; He will transform it. His new heaven and new earth will be qualitatively different:

- There will be no more tears (21:4). Sorrow, pain, and suffering shall be forgotten, and unimaginable joy will be our constant experience.
- The New Jerusalem will be a perfect place to dwell (21:16).
- The wall, over two hundred feet thick, will be crystal clear, indicating the city's purity (21:18).
- Only one street is mentioned, and it is pure gold (21:21).
- Jesus came as the Light of this world, so we should not be surprised that the glory of God and of the Lamb will provide the illumination in the New Jerusalem (21:23).
- The city gates are not closed because there will no longer be any enemies (21:25).

And He shall reign forever and ever!

HENRY & RICHARD BLACKABY | DISCOVERING GOD'S DAILY AGENDA

Jesus—the only One—makes:

God visible
Change possible
Happiness attainable
Resources ample
Suffering understandable
Sin forgivable
And heaven available.

ANNE GRAHAM LOTZ

MY JESUS IS...EVERYTHING

Our Hearts
Are *at* Rest

CONTENTMENT IS SOMETHING we must learn. It isn't a trait we're born with. But the question is how? In 1 Timothy 6 we find a couple of very practical answers to that question:

A current perspective on eternity: "For we have brought nothing into the world, so we cannot take anything out of it either" (v. 7).

A simple acceptance of essentials: "And if we have food and covering, with these we shall be content" (v. 8).

Both attitudes work beautifully. . . .

You see, society's plan of attack is to create dissatisfaction, to convince us that we must be in a constant pursuit for something "out there" that is sure to bring us happiness. When you reduce that lie to its lowest level, it is saying that contentment is impossible without striving for more.

God's Word offers the exact opposite advice: Contentment is possible when we stop striving for more. Contentment never comes from externals. Never!

As a Greek sage once put it: "To whom little is not enough, nothing is enough."

CHARLES SWINDOLL

THE FINISHING TOUCH

THE BOOK OF REVELATION COULD be entitled the Book of Home-coming, for in it we are given a picture of our heavenly home.

John's descriptions of the future steal your breath. His depiction of the final battle is graphic. Good clashes with evil. The sacred encounters the sinful. The pages howl with the shrieks of dragons and smolder with the coals of fiery pits. But in the midst of the battlefield there is a rose. John describes it in chapter 21:

Then I saw a new heaven and a new earth, for the first heaven and the first earth had passed away, and there was no longer any sea. I saw the Holy City, the new Jerusalem, coming down out of heaven from God, prepared as a bride beautifully dressed for her husband. . . .

In this final mountaintop encounter, God pulls back the curtain and allows the warrior to peek into the homeland. When given the task of writing down what he sees, John chooses the most beautiful comparison earth has to offer. The Holy City, John says, is like "a bride beautifully dressed for her husband."

MAX LUCADO | THE APPLAUSE OF HEAVEN

Rest on this earth is a false rest. Beware of those who urge you to find happiness here; you won't find it. Guard against the false physicians who promise that joy is only a diet away, a marriage away, a job away, or a transfer away. . . .

Try this. Imagine a perfect world. Whatever that means to you, imagine it. Does that mean peace? Then envision absolute tranquility. Does a perfect world imply joy? Then create your highest happiness. Will a perfect world have love? If so, ponder a place where love has no bounds. Whatever heaven means to you, imagine it. Get it firmly fixed in your mind. Delight in it. Dream about it. Long for it.

And then smile as the Father reminds you, *No one has ever imagined what God has prepared for those who love him.* . . .

When it comes to describing heaven, we are all happy failures.

Max Lucado | When God Whispers Your Name

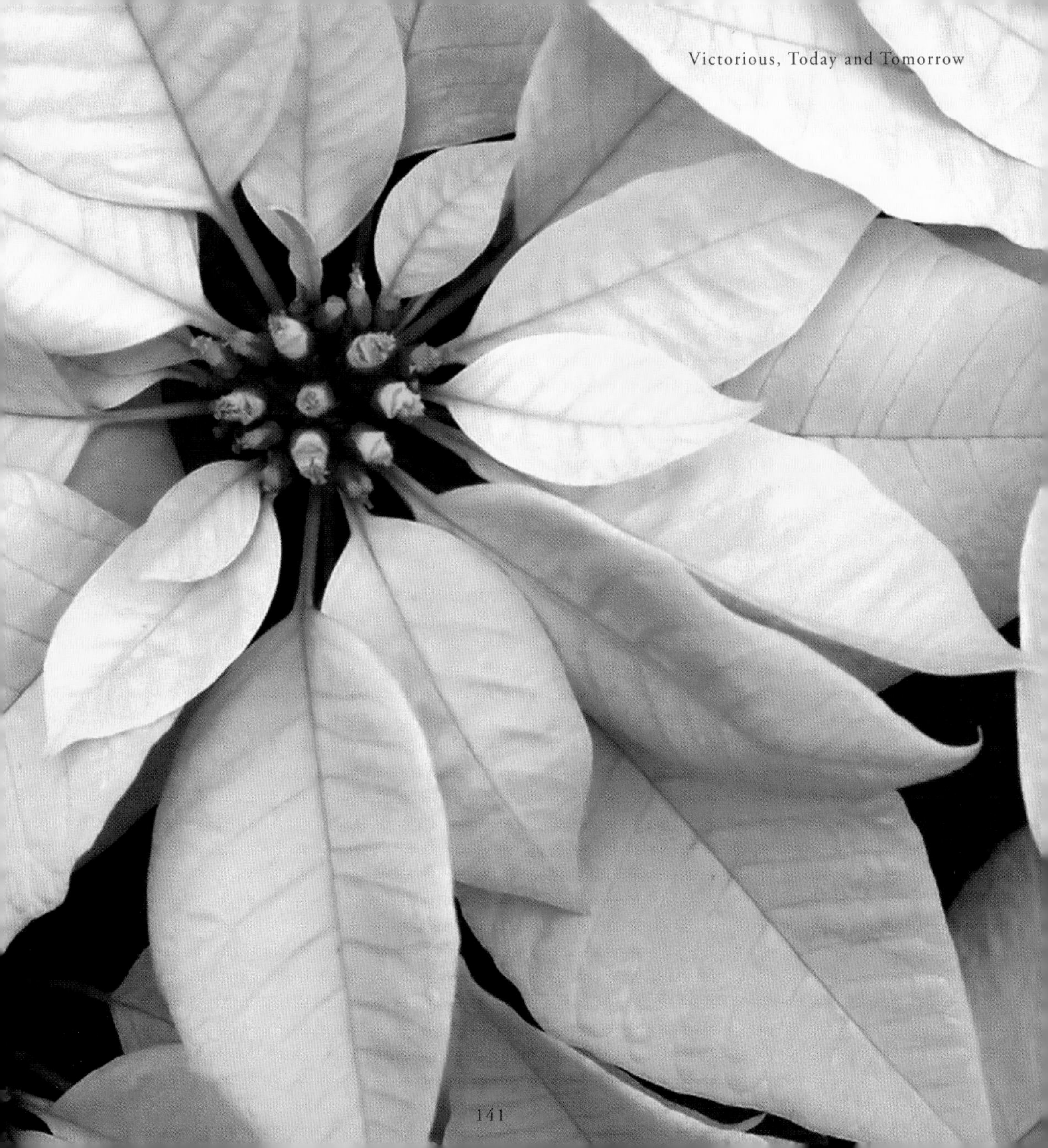

WHERE DID CHRISTIANS get the idea that we'd be appreciated, affirmed, and admired? The Savior himself taught that blessings are reserved for the persecuted, for those who are reviled, for those against whom folks say all kinds of evil . . . falsely . . . (Matthew 5:10–11). . . .

It sure is easy to forget those words and get soft, becoming too tender, too sensitive. Fragility is not a virtue extolled in Scripture. Saints with thin skin get distracted and, shortly thereafter, discouraged. There is a long, demanding course to be run, most of which takes place in the trenches and without applause. I suggest we lower our expectations as we intensify our determination and head for the goal.

Endurance is the secret, not popularity.

CHARLES SWINDOLL | THE FINISHING TOUCH

"There are many rooms in my father's house."

What a tender phrase. A house implies rest, safety, warmth, a table, a bed, a place to be at home. But this isn't just any house. It is our Father's house.

All of us know what it is like to be in a house that is not our own. Perhaps you've spent time in a dorm room or army barrack. Maybe you've slept in your share of hotels or bunked in a few hostels. They have beds. They have tables. They may have food and they may be warm, but they are a far cry from being "your father's house."

Your father's house is where your father is. . . .

We don't always feel welcome here on earth. We wonder if there is a place here for us. People can make us feel unwanted. Tragedy leaves us feeling like intruders. Strangers. Interlopers in a land not ours. We don't always feel welcome here.

We shouldn't. This isn't our home. To feel unwelcome is no tragedy. Indeed it is healthy. We are not home here. This language we speak, it's not ours. This body we wear, it isn't us. And the world we live in, this isn't home.

MAX LUCADO

A GENTLE THUNDER

ACKNOWLEDGMENTS

Grateful acknowledgment is made to the following publishers and copyright holders for permission to reprint copyrighted material:

MAX LUCADO

The Applause of Heaven. Dallas:Word. © Max Lucado, 1990, 1996.
When God Whispers Your Name. Dallas:Word. © Max Lucado, 1994.
A Gentle Thunder. Dallas:Word. © Max Lucado, 1995.
In the Grip of Grace. Dallas:Word. © Max Lucado, 1996.

CHARLES SWINDOLL

The Grace Awakening. Dallas: Word. © Charles Swindoll, 1990.
The Finishing Touch. Dallas: Word. © Charles Swindoll, 1994.
Flying Closer to the Flame. Dallas: Word. © Charles Swindoll, 1993, 1995.

ANNE GRAHAM LOTZ

Poetry | Some time ago, I received a homemade cassette tape with the handwritten title "My King Is…" From what I could gather, a man named Lockridge had been called to the platform during a church service to tell the congregation who his King is. The tape was a recording of his eloquent answer. In a rich voice that resonated with passion and increased in volume and tempo as he warmed to his subject, he thundered his description of his King, Jesus—in three minutes!

When the tape ended, I rewound it and replayed it. This unknown brother in Christ had absolutely thrilled my soul with his description of my King, Jesus!

I have taken Mr. Lockridge's idea—and, at times, some of his very phrases—and written descriptions of Jesus that appear throughout this book. Even as I pray that these descriptions of our King Jesus will be a blessing to you, I pray for Mr. Lockridge: God bless you always, sir, for the blessing you have been to this servant of the King!

My Jesus Is…Everything. J. Countryman®. © Anne Graham Lotz, 2005.

HENRY & RICHARD BLACKABY

Discovering God's Daily Agenda. Thomas Nelson®, Inc.
© Dr.'s Henry and Richard Blackaby, 2007.